LEADERS : BORN OR MADE
A guide to understand leadership and leaders and their work.

James BLESSING

CONTENT

Introduction

This section centers around the initiative, which is a more unique term and proposes a few components of a singular's style and values.

In the associations in which I have worked, "authority" has frequently come to mean the gathering, leaders maybe, that sits at the highest point of various leveled associations. These individuals are frequently saturated with administration by their situation. Nonetheless, according to the perspective of driving groundbreaking change, those in administrative roles could be viable pioneers.

Authority can be depicted essentially or with extraordinary intricacy. Essentially, it is driving an association or gathering. I have considered the definition to be basic as anybody with devotees; for instance, the local escort at the Acropolis. Pioneers have an impact. There is an idea of setting headings and simply deciding.

From a more intricate viewpoint, there have been studies and investigations of pioneers, initiative, and authority styles for quite a long time. Military pioneers and mentors of sports frequently top the rundown. There are numerous scientific categorizations of authority. There are businesses of showing authority and persuasive discourses by pioneers. The intricacy emerges because there are numerous people, many sorts of associations, and many kinds of objectives that require pioneers. There are numerous ways of accomplishing objectives. A few people are the right chief, with perfect timing, for a specific arrangement of objectives. At different times and for different objectives, they are not the right chief.

The initiative is the achievement of an objective through the heading of human colleagues. The one who effectively marshals his human partners to accomplish specific closures is a pioneer. An extraordinary pioneer can do so for a large number of days, and many years, in a wide assortment of conditions.

He may not have or show power; force or the danger of mischief might in all likelihood never go into his dealings. He may not be famous; his adherents might in all likelihood never do what he wishes out of adoration or reverence for him. He may not at any point be a vivid individual; he might in all likelihood never utilize important gadgets to sensationalize the reasons for his gathering or to zero in consideration on his authority. Concerning the significant matter of putting forth objectives, he might take care of the business of little impact, or even of little expertise; as a pioneer, he may just complete the plans of others.

His novel accomplishment is a human and social one that stems from how he might interpret his kindred laborers and the relationship of their singular objectives to the gathering objective that he should complete.

Issues and Deceptions

It isn't difficult to state in a couple of words what fruitful pioneers do that makes them compelling. Yet, it is a lot harder to coax out the parts that decide their prosperity. The standard strategy is to give satisfactory acknowledgment of every specialist's capability so he can predict the fulfillment of some significant interest or rationale of his in the doing of the gathering venture. Rough types of administration depend entirely on single wellsprings of fulfillment like money-related rewards or the lightening of fears about different sorts of uncertainty. The undertaking is stuck because following requests will prompt a check, and deviation will prompt joblessness.

Nobody can question that such types of inspiration are viable inside limits. Mechanically, they do join the laborer's circumstance to the interest of the business or the gathering. Yet, nobody can question the shortcomings of such basic methods. Individuals are not machines with a solitary arrangement of press buttons. At the point when their mind-boggling reactions to cherish, renown, autonomy, accomplishment, and gathering enrollment are unnoticed at work, they perform, best case scenario, as automata who bring undeniably not exactly their most extreme effectiveness to the undertaking, and even from a pessimistic standpoint as defiant slaves who deliberately or unknowingly harm the exercises they should further.

Unexpectedly, our fundamental picture of "the pioneer" is frequently to such an extent that of a tactical leader, because — more often than not, in any event — military associations are the most perfect illustration of an unoriginal use of straightforward prize and discipline as propelling gadgets. The creation in The Second Great War of the expression "mess" (circumstance typical, all messed up) only typifies what writing about military life from Greece and Rome to the current day has abundantly recorded; in particular, that in no other human undertaking is resolve commonly so poor or goldbricking and waste such a huge amount in proof.

CHAPTER 1

THINGS ABOUT LEADERS

The initiative is learned the way of behaving that becomes oblivious and programmed after some time. For instance, pioneers can settle on a few significant conclusions about an issue in the time it takes others to figure out the inquiry. Many individuals can't help thinking about how pioneers know how to settle on the most ideal choices, frequently under monstrous tension.

The most common way of pursuing these choices comes from a gathering of encounters and experiences with a large number of various conditions, character types, and unexpected disappointments. All the more thus, the dynamic cycle is an intense comprehension of being know all about the circumstances and logical results of conduct and conditional examples; knowing the insight and interconnection points of the factors engaged with these examples permits a pioneer to decide and extend the likelihood of their ideal results unhesitatingly.

The best chiefs are instinctual leaders. Having done it so often all through their professions, they become safe from the strain related to navigation and very instinctive about the method involved with pursuing the most key and ideal choices. To this end, most senior leaders will let you know they rely firmly on their "stomach feel" while pursuing hard decisions immediately.

Past navigation and effective administration across all areas become learned and instinctual throughout some time. Fruitful pioneers have taken in the dominance of expecting business designs, finding open doors in pressure circumstances, serving individuals they lead, and conquering difficulties. No big surprise the best Presidents are paid such a lot of cash.

Things you should do naturally, and consistently, to be an effective forerunner in the working environment and each spot

1. Encourage Others to Make some noise

Ordinarily, pioneers threaten their partners with their titles and power when they stroll into a room. Effective pioneers divert consideration away from themselves and urge others to voice their viewpoints. They are masters of encouraging others to make some noise and unhesitatingly share their viewpoints and perspectives. They utilize their leader presence to establish an agreeable climate.

2. Decide

Effective pioneers are master chefs. They either work with the discourse to enable their partners to arrive at an essential resolution or they do it without anyone's help. They center around "getting things going" consistently - dynamic exercises that support progress. Fruitful pioneers have become amazing at politicking and consequently don't throw away their energy on issues that disturb force. They know how to go with 30 choices in a short time.

3. Convey Assumptions

Fruitful pioneers are extraordinary communicators, and this is particularly obvious utter your " execution assumptions." In doing as such, they help their partners to remember the association's guiding principle and statement of purpose - guaranteeing that their vision is appropriately deciphered and noteworthy targets are appropriately executed.

I had a manager that dealt with the group by helping us to remember the assumptions that she had of the gathering. She made it simple for the group to remain on track and on target. The convention she executed - by obviously imparting assumptions - expanded execution and assisted with distinguishing those in the group that couldn't stay aware of the guidelines she anticipated from us.

4. Challenge Individuals to Think

The best chiefs grasp their associates' outlooks, capacities, and regions for development. They utilize this information/knowledge to provoke their groups to think and stretch them to go after more. These kinds of pioneers succeed in keeping their kin honest, never permitting them to settle in and empowering them with the devices to develop.

On the off chance that you are not thinking, you're not learning new things. On the off chance that you're not learning, you're not developing - and after some time becoming superfluous in your work.

5. Be Responsible to Other people

Effective pioneers permit their partners to oversee them. This doesn't mean they are permitting others to control them - but instead becoming responsible to guarantee they are being proactive to their associate's requirements.

Past tutoring and supporting chosen representatives, and being responsible to others is an indication that your chief is centered more around your prosperity than simply your own.

6. Show others how it's done

Showing others how it's done sounds simple, yet a couple of pioneers are predictable with this one. Effective pioneers try to do what they say others should do and are aware of their activities. They realize everybody is watching them and in this manner are unquestionably natural about distinguishing the people who are noticing everything they might do, standing by to identify a presentation deficit.

7. Measure and Award Execution

Extraordinary pioneers generally have major areas of strength for business execution and those individuals who are the presentation champions. Besides the fact that they audit the numbers and measure execution return for capital invested, however, they are likewise dynamic in recognizing difficult work and endeavors (regardless of the outcome). Fruitful pioneers never underestimate predictable entertainers and are aware of remunerating them.

8. Give Constant Criticism

Workers believe their chiefs should realize that they are focusing on them and they value any bits of knowledge en route. Fruitful pioneers generally give criticism and they invite corresponding input by making dependable associations with their partners. They figure out the force of viewpoint and have taken in the significance of criticism from the beginning in their profession as it has served them to empower the working environment headway.

9. Appropriately Apportion and Send Ability

Effective pioneers realize their ability pool and how to utilize it. They are seasoned veterans of initiating the capacities of their partners and knowing when to send their extraordinary ranges of abilities given the conditions within reach.

10. Get clarification on pressing issues, Look for Direction

Effective pioneers clarify some pressing issues and look for counsel constantly. From an external perspective, they seem, by all accounts, to be know-everything - yet within, they have a profound hunger for information and continually are keeping watch to learn new things as a result of their obligation to improve themselves through the insight of others.

11. Issue Address; Keep away from Delaying

Fruitful pioneers tackle gives head-on and knows how to find the main issue in question. They don't linger and in this way become extraordinarily capable of critical thinking; they gain from and don't keep away from awkward conditions (they invite them).

Excelling in life is tied in with doing the things that a great many people could do without doing.

12. Positive Energy and Disposition

Effective pioneers make a positive and rousing working environment culture. They know how to establish the vibe and bring a disposition that propels their partners to make a move. In that capacity, they are affable, regarded, serious areas of strength for and. They don't permit disappointments to upset energy.

13. Be an Extraordinary Educator

Numerous representatives in the work environment will let you know that their chiefs have quit being educators. Fruitful pioneers teach constantly because they are so self-propelled to learn themselves. They use instructing to keep their partners all around educated and proficient through insights, patterns, and other newsworthy things.

Effective pioneers set aside some margin to coach their associates and make the venture to support the people who have demonstrated they are capable and anxious to progress.

14. Put resources into Connections

Effective pioneers don't zero in on safeguarding their area - all things being equal, they extend it by putting resources into commonly gainful connections. Effective pioneers partner themselves with "lifters and different pioneers" - the kinds of individuals that can widen their range of authority. For their progression as well as that of others.

Pioneers share the gathering of their prosperity to assist with gathering speed for people around them.

15. Truly Appreciate Liabilities

Effective pioneers love being pioneers - not for power but rather for the significant and intentional effect they can make. At the point when you have arrived at a senior degree of initiative - it's about your capacity to serve others and this can't be achieved except if you appreciate what you do.

Eventually, effective pioneers can support their prosperity because these 15 things, at last, permit them to expand the worth of their association's image - while simultaneously limiting the working gamble profile. They act as the empowering influences of ability, culture, and results

CHAPTER 2

IDENTIFYING TYPES OF LEADERS

The 5 most normal initiative styles and how to see as yours and characterize your chief

From the beginning of time, incredible pioneers have arisen each with specific initiative styles
Administration in itself is a fairly liquid rule. By and large, most pioneers adjust their styles to suit what is going on. This is especially obvious the more they lead, as they learn and draw in with their representatives they adjust their authority style.

To turn into an additional effective pioneer, pioneers need to comprehend where they are as of now. In this article, we'll make sense of what an initiative style is, then, at that point, take a gander at 5 of the most well-known authority styles and how powerful they are.

Groundbreaking Initiative
Delegative Authority
Definitive Initiative
Value-based Initiative
Participative Authority
What is an initiative style?
An initiative style alludes to a pioneer's strategies, qualities, and ways of behaving while coordinating, rousing, and dealing with their groups.

Their authority style is likewise the deciding variable in how pioneers foster their technique, carry out plans and answer changes while dealing with the assumptions of partners and the prosperity of their group.

As you begin to think about a portion of individuals who you consider extraordinary pioneers, you can quickly see that there are much of the time tremendous contrasts in how every individual leads.

For what reason is it vital to realize your authority style?
As a pioneer, understanding your initiative style is significant. At the point when you truly do comprehend your administration style, you can decide the impact this has on those that you straightforwardly impact.

A few chiefs are now ready to sort their ongoing initiative style, perceiving whether this makes them powerful pioneers. Or on the other hand how their workers see them. However, it isn't generally so characterized. It is normally the situation that pioneers can classify their style, but frequently will generally show qualities of numerous other initiative styles too.

One simple method for understanding what your authority style is involved criticism. Asking the people who you lead to furnishing you with transparent criticism is a useful activity. Doing so will permit you to adjust your style's qualities to your everyday obligations as a pioneer.

Prepared to find your authority style?

1. Groundbreaking authority
We've probably totally been in a gathering circumstance where somebody assumed command, speaking with the gathering and making a common vision. Making solidarity, creating bonds, making energy, and imparting enthusiasm. This individual is probably going to be considered a groundbreaking chief.

Groundbreaking initiative is an initiative style that underscores change and change. Pioneers who embrace this approach endeavor to move their devotees to accomplish more than they at any point expected by taking advantage of their true capacity. This sort of authority can be very successful in associations that are hoping to roll out significant improvements or changes.

A portion of the vital qualities of a groundbreaking initiative include:

An emphasis on what's to come: Groundbreaking pioneers are continuously looking forward and pondering how should be accomplished the association's objectives. They rouse their adherents to do likewise.

An emphasis on change: Groundbreaking pioneers are OK with the change and comprehend that it is vital for hierarchical achievement. They work to guarantee that their devotees are likewise alright with change and can adjust to it.

An emphasis on individuals: Groundbreaking pioneers see the expected in all of their supporters. They endeavor to foster their adherents' assets and capacities so they can arrive at their maximum capacity.

2. Delegative authority
Frequently alluded to as "free enterprise", a delegated authority style centers around designating drive to colleagues. This is by and large known as one of the most un-meddlesome types of administration, this means "let them do". This is thusly thought to be a very hands-off initiative style.

Pioneers who take on this style have trust, depending on their workers to go about their responsibilities. They don't constantly hover over or get too engaged with giving criticism or direction. All things considered, delegative pioneers allow their workers to use their imagination, assets, and experience to assist them with meeting their objectives.

This can be an effective initiative methodology if colleagues are capable and get a sense of ownership of their work. Nonetheless, delegative initiative can likewise prompt conflicts among colleagues and may part or separate a gathering.

It tends to be especially hard for newbies to adjust to this style of administration, or for staff individuals to foster comprehension of who is eventually in control and liable for results. Along these lines, this authority style should be held within proper limits.

3. Definitive initiative

Definitive pioneers are frequently alluded to as visionary. Pioneers who embrace this style view themselves as guides to their supporters. In no way related to dictator initiative, legitimate administration puts more accentuation on a "follow me" approach. Along these lines, pioneers graph a course and urge people around them to follow.

Pioneers who show definitive characteristics will quite often propel and move people around them. As they give generally speaking bearing, they likewise give direction, criticism, and inspiration to their groups. This advances a feeling of achievement or accomplishment.

The legitimate initiative style depends vigorously on getting to know every individual from a group. This permits a pioneer to give direction and input on a more customized level, assisting people with succeeding. This implies legitimate pioneers should have the option to adjust, especially as the size of their group develops.

Legitimate authority is very active, yet pioneers should practice alert not to continuously hover over. This is a propensity with this style, which can be oppressive to colleagues and make negative opinions.

4. Conditional administration

The conditional initiative frequently alluded to as administrative administration, is an initiative style that depends on remunerations and disciplines. This initiative style has an unmistakable accentuation on structure, expecting people may not have the inspiration expected to follow through with their responsibilities.

With this prize-based framework, a pioneer lays out clear objectives or undertakings for their groups. Pioneers likewise clarify how their groups will be compensated (or rebuffed) for their work. Prizes can take many configurations however normally will include monetary rewards, like compensation, or a reward.

This "compromise" authority style is more worried about effectively following laid out schedules and methodology, than with making any groundbreaking changes to an association.

Conditional authority lays out jobs and responsibilities for every worker. Notwithstanding, it can prompt consistent losses assuming representatives are generally mindful of how much their work is worth. Subsequently, it is vital that impetuses are steady with organization objectives and upheld by extra tokens of appreciation.

5. Participative authority
In some cases alluded to as just initiative, the participative initiative is an administration style empowering pioneers to pay attention to their workers and include them in the dynamic cycle. This authority style expects pioneers to be comprehensive, use great relational abilities, and urgently, have the option to share power/obligation.

The point when a pioneer embraces a participative style of initiative, energizes cooperation, through responsibility. This frequently prompts an aggregate exertion of a group to distinguish issues and foster arrangements, instead of doling out individual faults.

This administration style has generally been extremely normal and used by a large number of pioneers in numerous associations. Notwithstanding, as working propensities have changed and groups have become more decentralized it makes this initiative style more troublesome.

Unconstrained, open, and real correspondence is frequently connected with a participative initiative style. Remote working or virtual groups can make this especially difficult to keep up with.

Participative authority is frequently preferred as it assists with building entrust with workers. Enabling them and empowering them to share their thoughts on significant issues, showing their worth to a group.

CHAPTER 3

ARE LEADERS BORN OR MADE?

“Great pioneers are brought into the world with inborn qualities and attributes anyway incredible pioneers are made through their day-to-day intentional and tenacious activities, educational encounters, constant learning, and self-improvement rehearse."

Are pioneers conceived or made? This is an inquiry many are as yet scratching their heads over looking for the right response. I'm composing this article after having done an exploration on the point to impart to you. From my encounters, I have seen that a have a characteristic tendency to lead, notwithstanding, a larger part of us have figured out how to lead through our encounters.

As per a concentrate on hereditary impacts on pioneers, 70% of the initiative is learnable. This infers that extraordinary pioneers advance as they go. The standard expresses that the way to dominate expertise is practice, and It is undoubtedly that we as a whole become better the more we practice however practice surely doesn't precisely mean flawlessness. Nor could we at any point method or evaluate the hours it will take us to turn into a specialist at an action or assignment.

Essentially because our capacity to learn and comprehend shifts given the qualities and characteristics we are brought into the world with. Allow me likewise to add that you don't need to be a specialist to be a pioneer.

Ability Versus Expertise

Ability is characterized as an intrinsic and exceptional capacity of an individual to follow through with something. An ability is a skill, which is obtained by an individual through learning. Ability is our God-gifted capacity, while expertise is a capacity where you put your time and work to create. Our capacities and ability alone are not what make us incredible pioneers. The administration is shown through our way of behaving and activities. Pioneers who center around further developing their great social characteristics are result arranged, as well as influence their abilities and abilities will undoubtedly find lasting success in creating different pioneers and driving effective associations.

Authority Through Situation

We should likewise consider the way that pioneers are not made by some coincidence. They are conceived and created by the situation. An extraordinary illustration of a lady who came to a position of authority through a situation is Yaa Asantewaa, the Sovereign Mother of Ejisu in the Ashanti district in Ghana, West Africa. She took on the influential position and became popular for driving the Ashanti insubordination to English expansionism to shield the Brilliant stool; an image of the Ashanti Realm. Before that job, she was at that point a firstborn kid, which requires a degree of initiative, and all through her life, she fostered her abilities with the different driving positions she procured before taking on her greatest driving job later on. History lets us know that she was picked by a few provincial Asante rulers to be the conflict head of the Asante battling force with a multitude of 5,000 individuals.

"Is it genuine that the valiance of the Ashanti is no more? I can barely handle it. It can't be! I should say this if you the men of Ashanti won't go ahead, then, at that point, we will. We the ladies will. I will call upon my kindred ladies... We will battle till the remainder of us falls on the combat zones."

Yaa Asantewaa's demonstration of valiance and initiative involved purposeful expertise and information. She was self-persuaded and ready to lead a gathering with a shared objective to protect the Ashanti Realm.

These were individuals she had the option to impact to join her during the unrest. Our natural interactive abilities are an adequate asset for collaborating, impacting, and connecting with others, which thus are the activities expected to oversee ability successfully. Superior workers needn't bother with to be roused, as self-inspiration is another innate asset we have, and the level of correspondence is the fundamental hotspot for overseeing really by and large. Thusly, imparting adequately, showing compassion towards others, and having the option to peruse the state of mind of your subordinates go quite far to being a decent pioneer as of now.

Martin Luther Lord Jr. is one more illustration of an incredible person with a conceived gift to lead individuals. He had an incredible capacity to get individuals to cooperate for a reachable objective. He could calm groups and quiet them down to be more tranquil and he by and large talked about peacefulness as the improved goal much of the time. Martin Luther Ruler was a pioneer since he shook things up. He had the boldness and certainty to defend what he put stock in, the freedoms, all things considered, to fair and approach treatment.

I have a fantasy that my four young kids will one day live in a country where they won't be decided by the shade of their skin, but by the substance of their personality.

We as a whole have the stuff to be extraordinary forerunners in the present globalized universe of self-learning and self-improvement. Authority attributes are inborn, implying that incredible pioneers are conceived and will arise when they are faced with suitable car circumstances and educational encounters. These people have specific characteristics and gifts, like profound trustworthiness, moral vision, sympathy, and care that make them appropriate for incredible authority.

Figuring out how to Lead

Pioneers can for sure be created, and initiative can be educated and rehearsed. People can get familiar with the abilities to be exceptional pioneers through life encounters and initiative advancement programs. Administration ought to be taken a gander at as an apprenticeship exchange. Figuring out how to be a pioneer is tied in with watching different pioneers and copying their way of behaving. As they carry on with life, potential pioneers will search out guides to show them how to deal with circumstances and become incredible pioneers. They will improve from input that they get from people around them and advance by evaluating new strategies and sorting out what will work and what won't work for them.

Potential pioneers advance by condemning their exhibition in circumstances and any disappointment is just a disappointment on the off chance that they don't gain from the experience. This is the way powerful pioneers control their predeterminations. They assume command over their turn of events and utilize the preparation of amazing open doors that are accessible to them. They utilize these preparation projects to take care of business and to gain from all of their encounters.

"Being a pioneer resembles being a man . If you need to remind individuals you will be, you're not.

Genuine authority is about validness and going to bat for standards even areas of strength for despite. The valid initiative is a result of genuineness. Trustworthiness is tied in with putting the requirements of others in front of your own. Trustworthiness in conveying data, both positive and negative.

All things considered, pioneers are both conceived and made. Many individuals normally have a few inward qualities and inclinations that make them bound to turn out to be great pioneers. Be that as it may, without difficult work and intentional leveling up of one's authority abilities the regular ability and inborn interactive abilities are probably not going to contribute towards fruitful extraordinary administration.

NOW THE QUESTION IS...WHO IS A LEADER?

PONDER YOUR POINTS HERE., ...

READERS SHOT NOTE :

www.ingramcontent.com/pod-product-compliance
Lightning Source LLC
LaVergne TN
LVHW080600160826
845677LV00010B/1938

* 9 7 9 8 3 5 1 6 0 9 2 0 1 *